Gold Mine in the Sky

Gold Mine in the Sky

A Personal History of the Log Cabin Mine

FRANK CASSIDY JR., DVM

iUniverse, Inc.
New York   Bloomington

Gold Mine in the Sky
A Personal History of the Log Cabin Mine

Copyright © 2010 Frank Cassidy Jr., DVM

iUniverse books may be ordered through booksellers or by contacting:

iUniverse
1663 Liberty Drive
Bloomington, IN 47403
www.iuniverse.com
1-800-Authors (1-800-288-4677)

ISBN: 978-1-4502-4691-0 (pbk)
ISBN: 978-1-4502-4692-7 (ebk)

Printed in the United States of America

iUniverse rev. date: 9/15/2010

Dedicated to the memory of
Frank Cassidy Sr. and Carol Cassidy,
who symbolized the Log Cabin Mine

Map of the Log Cabin Mine in relation to the
surrounding area (Courtesy of Eric Knight)

The Mono Basin, which is located on the rugged eastern slope of the High Sierra Mountains, is rich in mining history with such places as Bodie, the May-Lundy Mine, and Aurora, Nevada.

Sitting alone high above Mono Lake at an elevation of 10,000 feet is the Log Cabin Mine, guarded by its sentinel, the rugged Lee Vining Peak (11,696 ft.).

What remains of the once proud Log Cabin Mine are decaying buildings and equipment ravaged by both time and vandals.

To the people who were fortunate to work in the mine and all the people in the Mono Basin and beyond who feel connected to the Log Cabin Mine, this is still a magical place.

The Log Cabin Mine and the immediate surrounding area is closed to the public. Mercury contamination of the soil poses a definite health threat.

Lee Vining Peak (Cassidy Family Archives)

Contents

Acknowledgments and Special Dedication

I refer to my special wife, Robin Cassidy, throughout this personal history. She is my continual source of love and inspiration and has been for more than thirty years. Whether it be walking together through Robin's Grove on our way up to the Log Cabin Mine or helping me at the computer for many long hours on this project, she is always by my side, providing support.

I believe that she is as spiritually connected to the Mono Basin and the Log Cabin Mine as I am.

I know that her mom and guardian angel, Carol Cassidy Bauer, along with Frank Cassidy Sr. are smiling down on her.

After the first showing of *From Mine To Mint* at the Lee Vining U.S. Forest Service Visitor Center, Vineca Hess pointed her finger at me and said, "You have got to write a book," and I said "Oh sure!" However, after giving it some thought, it was really something I wanted to do. Rather, it was something I had to do! It became a passion. I must truly thank Vineca for igniting the spark.

I think that it is possible that at this point in time, August Hess and I are the only two people left who actually worked underground at the Log Cabin Mine. (Augie probably performed much more work than I did.)

This book turned into a long, major project, but it was truly a labor of love.

Needless to say, the book would not be possible without all the people who were connected to the Log Cabin Mine and made it special. I thank them from my heart.

I received so much help and encouragement during this project. I must thank Jane Freeburg, Debbe Eilts, Jon Kazmierski, Don Banta, Lily Mathieu La Braque, Norm De Chambeau, and Elmer "Buddy" Bayer Jr. among many others for their enthusiastic help. Mike and June of Digital Dreemz restored the quality of many of my photos.

Thanks go to Eric Knight for his reproducing the magical Log Cabin Mine in his sketches and also his professional map of the Log Cabin Mine region.

Thank you to my daughter-in-law, Stephanie, for improving on some poor-quality photos. She also enlisted the aid of Kelli Baptista, who transformed my amateurish attempt to draw a map depicting the special places of the Log Cabin Mine to an accurate and enjoyable illustration.

I give special thanks to my "hard editor" Kristin (Cassidy) Godfredsen, who does this sort of thing for a living and who gave her valuable time and expertise to her dad. She and I spent long hours editing this text, and without her, this book would not be, in her words, "a great read." Kristin is part of my lifeline, which is my family. Thank you!

My family is truly my lifeline. Without all five of my children, I would have never had the inspiration to attempt to write this book. Elizabeth, Kristin, Scott, Jim, and Nick have all embraced the Mono Basin and the rich history of the Log Cabin Mine. It gives me great pleasure to know that all the children and their families will perpetuate my passion for the Log Cabin Mine.

A special thanks go to my sister, Kathleen, and my cousin Pat for sharing their stories and remembrances of years in Lee Vining and the Log Cabin Mine and also sharing some precious family photographs.

Foreword

Gold Mine in the Sky: A Personal History of the Log Cabin Mine

This book is a complete and factual presentation of much of the interesting and early history of many, many events that were involved in the beginning or discovery of gold in this area of the High Sierras, and of the happenings that have taken place there soon after.

The author, Frank C. Cassidy Jr., DVM, is very qualified in giving a factual and interesting history. He is a very intelligent and interesting individual as well as being completely aware of the discovery and development of that part of the Sierra Nevada range of mountains, as well as surrounding mentioned places.

I have known Frank C. Cassidy Jr., DVM, from his early childhood and from his spending time at the Log Cabin Mine. He has presented in this book a vast treasure of knowledge and events that have taken place. You will find pleasure in reading his book.

Don Banta
Historian
Lifetime member of The Mono Basin Historical Society

Introduction

I was inspired to write this book after my involvement with the project that resulted in the movie *The Log Cabin Mine, From Mine to Mint*, which first showed in the theater at the USFS Visitors Center in Lee Vining, California, in the fall of 2009. When I was at the mine with the filmmakers, I found that they enjoyed the stories of my parents, my experiences growing up, and the details about gold mining seemingly as much as my family does. This made me realize that many others may be interested in these tales as well and that a book would be the best way to share this history.

It is my sincere hope that you, the reader, enjoy getting to know the many people and their experiences at the Log Cabin Mine. Writing this book was definitely a labor of love for me, and I am happy to share it with you.

As you will see, my father, Frank Cassidy Sr., along with his constant helpmate and wife, Carol (Keith) Cassidy, really were the Log Cabin Mine, from its inception in 1939 until Frank Sr.'s passing in 1968. I include some of their experiences away from the mine to demonstrate that it was the character and makeup of these two very special people who made the Log Cabin Mine a magical place. I was lucky to be along during a good portion of that ride, and I am pleased to share it with you now.

Early History

In 1890, a mining claim was filed in Mono County as the Mendocino claim. This claim would initiate a fascinating mining history spanning nearly a century. The claim would eventually become the Log Cabin Mine.

The Mono Basin is rich in mining history with such operations as Bodie and the Lundy Canyon Mine. A pictorial of the mining history of this area is available in the U.S. Forest Service Visitor Center in Lee Vining, California, but my intention here is to tell the history of the Log Cabin Mine and to bring to life the experience shared by the miners and their families.

In 1909, JT Hammond added his name to the Mendocino claim. Mr. Hammond founded the Hammond's Store on the shores of Mono Lake in 1907. He had numerous mining claims in the area. Mr. Hammond's store eventually became the Tioga Lodge. To this day, it is still in the same spot on beautiful Mono Lake.

In 1910–1911, a miner named Jim Simpson re-filed on the original Mendocino claim and it became the Simpson Mine. Thus began the long and fascinating history that leads up to and includes the Log Cabin Mine.

Imagine Jim Simpson bringing supplies and equipment by horseback almost straight up the canyon behind Hammond's Store to his mine. This was about a three-thousand-foot climb as the mine was at an elevation of ten thousand feet. The Simpson brothers and associates worked the mine from 1910 to 1930—twenty years!

Hammond's store with Tioga Canyon in the background—Jim Simpson's original trail to the mine. (Courtesy of Mono Basin Historical Society)

Jim Simpson's old cabin.

The Simpsons sold the mine to Mutual Gold in 1930, which triggered an increase in activity. Structures and buildings were built, people were hired, and processing at the mine picked up pace.

This was dangerous country, especially in the winter. Take for example the two miners Dan Callahan (age sixty) and Mickey Sullivan (age thirty). They had snowshoed down from the mine to Lee Vining, a distance of about five miles, to celebrate Saint Patrick's Day, circa 1936, at Bodie Mike's Saloon. The celebration lasted the weekend, and against all advice, they decided to head back to the mine in the middle of a fierce snowstorm. They did not want to be AWOL from the mine and risk being laid off. Ironically and tragically, they were found frozen to death on their holiday attempting to get back to the mine.

This was still rough country even in the non-winter months. Darius De Chambeau worked at the mine circa 1938–1939. He, along with other miners, would leave their families in Lee Vining and hike straight up the hill behind the town and up to the mine on Monday mornings in time to go to work. This was at least a three-thousand-foot elevation change. The men would stay in the mine bunkhouse during the work week before returning to Lee Vining.

This information comes from Darius's son, Norman, who is the curator of the Mono Basin Historical Society at the old schoolhouse in Lee Vining.

The De Chambeau family first settled in the Mono Basin in the late nineteenth century. They homesteaded land on which they both ranched and farmed. They produced much of the meat and vegetables that were badly needed by the miners and their families.

During one shift at the mine, Darius slipped on a muddy surface and fell into a conveyor belt that was carrying ore to a rock crusher, crushing his arm between the belt and the rollers. Fortunately, another worker heard his screams and shut down the conveyor. Darius was loaded onto the back of an old truck and transported down the Log Cabin Mine Road for a quick stop at Lee Vining before heading for West Portal, where local doctors stabilized him. He was rushed to Los Angeles, where doctors somehow saved his arm and hand with many skin grafts. Darius regained full use of his hand except for one finger that remained pointing up stiffly in the air. Darius worked hard the rest of his ninety-six years, and it is reported that his only regret was that it was the wrong finger that remained stiff!

Rough country demanded rough people. They had to be tough!

Norman De Chambeau, curator of the Mono Basin Historical Society at the
Old Schoolhouse Museum at Lee Vining, CA. (Cassidy Family Archives)

Gus Hess, remembered as the "Father of Lee Vining," and his brother, Bill, hauled most of the material and equipment up the steep and rocky five-mile Log Cabin Mine Road. Augie Hess, one of Gus's sons, worked in the mine as a mucker and as a driver hauling material to the mine.

Gus and Bill actually did the majority of the construction at the mine. Many of those buildings and the original gallis frame are still there today. By way of definition, the gallis frame is a pivotal structure required in any gold mining operation. It is a tall wooden structure that houses a wheel at the top. The cable that is attached to the top of the skip runs around this wheel and down to the hoist drum in the hoist house. The *skip* is the mining term used for the cage that lifts and lowers men and equipment in the mine shaft. Additional details on the structures and science of gold mining are provided in later chapters.

The gallis frame at the Log Cabin Mine. You can just glimpse the top of the skip at the bottom. (Cassidy Family Archives)

The skip in later years. Safety precautions were taken
sometime after 1971. (Picture source is unknown)

In the forties, when Gus was hauling equipment to the mine, he was kind enough to take me along as his helper, or swamper, as he called me. I was only a little kid, but I can still remember the front end of that truck bouncing up and down as Gus geared down for the sheep corral grade (37 percent and the steepest section of the Log Cabin Mine Road). I was too young to be scared, but Augie still remembers feeling the adrenaline as the front end of his truck jolted up and down on that steep grade as he hauled material to the mine.

One of Gus's original trucks. I was his swamper. (Cassidy Family Archives)

Bill (left) and Gus Hess (known as the "Father of Lee Vining") in
1929, overlooking Lee Vining Canyon. (Courtesy of Vineca Hess)

Mutual Gold continued to work the mine in the thirties and expanded
the property by filing additional claims in the name of the Simpson Mine.
In 1939, the mine was purchased by Frank Garbutt. He made many vital
improvements at a significant cost. He spent in excess of ninety thousand
dollars (probably millions in today's dollars) to run a power line up Tioga
Canyon to the mine, to upgrade the ball mill to accommodate greater tonnage
and to add a modern hoist and an Ingersoll Rand air compressor. This was
the beginning of the Log Cabin Mine.

Frank Garbutt. (Picture source is unknown)

The Ingersoll Rand air compressor. (Cassidy Family Archives)

The mine sub station, due to Frank Garbutt. (Courtesy of MBHS)

View inside the hoist house, showing the drum, the wheel
indicating the levels to the operator, the clutch and brake levers,
and the operator's chair. (Cassidy Family Archives)

An Adventuresome Pair

To truly understand the life and history of the Log Cabin Mine, it is important to know the background of the people who made it the success that it was: my parents.

My father, Frank Coleman Cassidy, was born in Philadelphia, Pennsylvania, in 1910, and he lived there until high school graduation in 1927.

In 1926, at the age of sixteen, my father took a course in physical science from instructor George Rosengarten at Philadelphia Boy's High School. I am fortunate to have his notebook from that course, and I am amazed at the complexity and depth of that subject. I have taken physics classes at the University of California that were not as difficult or complex.

My dad's father, my grandfather (or Pop-Pop as he was known) was the athletic trainer at the University of Pennsylvania and a man beloved by the athletes. I have many letters to him documenting their admiration and affection. However, the family decided that they wanted to move west, and so Pop-Pop took a position as the athletic trainer at Chaffey College in California.

A sample of Dad's work. (Cassidy Family Archives)

My father became a self-made man. It did not hurt that he was "one handsome devil" (as my mom liked to say). He was a true Renaissance man: physically strong, not afraid of hard work, intelligent, and highly inquisitive about all subjects, especially mining.

Already a handsome devil at age ten. (Cassidy Family Archives)

Frank Sr. as a young man, 1932. (Cassidy Family Archives)

My mother, Carol (Keith) Cassidy, graduated from Hollywood High School, and her class was the first to hold their graduation ceremony in the Hollywood Bowl.

It was a memorable event for my mom, a tall, fair-skinned, beautiful woman with piercing blue eyes, as her height required her to stand in the back row with the tall boys. My mom, who had a special talent for finding the best in any situation, always delighted in relating this story to her children and grandchildren through the years.

My father's interest in mining led him to a seminar in Los Angeles where he met David Keith, Carol's father, who introduced him to his daughter, Martha Carolyn. This was the beginning of many "seminars" (supervised, of course) between Frank Cassidy and Martha Carolyn Keith—Carol.

Mom, already sophisticated at age seven. (Cassidy Family Archives)

My parents were married in 1933 in Los Angeles, California. Being the adventuresome pair they were, my mom and dad ventured to Virginia City, Nevada. At the age of twenty-three, my father started working in the mines, where he honed his skills and gained his initial experiences in mining.

Frank Sr. and Carol Cassidy on their wedding day,
October 2, 1933. (Cassidy Family Archives)

Frank Sr. and Carol Cassidy in Virginia City, Nevada,
circa 1933. (Cassidy Family Archives)

My parents lived in a small rented house in Virginia City during the last days of Prohibition in 1933. The house had few amenities, but it did have a basement that came in handy for the local bootleggers who had befriended my father while working in the mines. The bootleggers somehow knew when the revenuers were coming. (The revenuers were federal agents who would search for illegal supplies of liquor during Prohibition.) The bootleggers, in order to outsmart the revenuers, would hide their supply of liquor in my parents' basement. After all, who would suspect a nice, clean-cut couple of supporting this illegal activity? After the revenuers left empty-handed, my parents were usually treated to a sample of Virginia City gold in the liquid form.

My mom and dad would, from time to time, make the sixty-mile round trip to visit the biggest little city in the world, Reno, Nevada. The trip involved going down the infamous Geiger Grade. This is one of the steepest grades on Nevada highways and is even a challenge for today's vehicles with modern breaking systems. But in the thirties, a little ingenuity was all that my mother and father needed to overcome any obstacle. To supplement their brakes on the most dangerous parts of the grade, my father would use a long chain to attach a big log to the back of their vehicle. This "emergency brake" provided enough weight to make the downhill speeds manageable.

When we took my mom to visit Virginia City years later, we made the drive down the grade in a 4x4 SUV. We listened to her recall this story and were awestruck with admiration as we navigated our way down, barely trusting our manufacturer-supplied brakes. Our entire family always enjoys the story about the log dragged behind the car, and we can't make the trip without remembering it.

Between 1933 and 1938 in Virginia City, my dad worked in several mines; some were very deep. It would get smoldering hot at the lower levels, and the work shifts had to be shortened because of the heat. During this time period, my father actually filed a mining claim of his own and did initial work and research to locate and process gold. Perhaps it was here that his quest for knowledge and information began—and never stopped. He continued his education in mining all through his life. I can remember years later seeing his quarters at the Log Cabin Mine: a neatly made bed and full bookshelves. I believe that anything one wanted to know about mining could be found in those books and also inside my father's head. The long winter nights he spent at the mine during the week were not wasted.

In early 1938, my parents, Frank and Carol, left the adventuresome life in Virginia City and returned to Los Angeles to be close to family. It was time to begin the whole new adventure of parenthood. I was born in Hollywood Hospital on April 30, 1938.

Mom and me in 1938. (Cassidy Family Archives)

From Los Angeles to the
Log Cabin Mine

In 1939, my father answered an ad in the *Los Angeles Times*. Frank Garbutt was looking for a superintendent to run his recently purchased Log Cabin Mine. My father, at the age of twenty-nine, already had extensive mining experience from his years working in Virginia City, Nevada.

Mr. Garbutt was a wealthy Los Angeles industrialist and entrepreneur who had multiple mining properties. Among his many holdings and assets was the Los Angeles Athletic Club. Mr. Garbutt had an interest in amateur athletics, especially boxing.

My father and Mr. Garbutt hit it off immediately, but a job interview was required. Mr. Garbutt had arranged an exhibition boxing match between my father and Mickey Walker (then middleweight champion of the world). Perhaps this was to see if my father was up to the task of handling seventy-two miners working three shifts around the clock at ten thousand feet elevation. Apparently, my father passed the test because Mr. Garbutt hired him as his superintendent in 1939, and a strong mutual respect was formed. Frank Sr. and Carol, married for six years and with an infant son, were ready for their trip to the Log Cabin Mine.

The First Year, The Toughest Year

In the spring of 1940, my father packed up his young family and made the long trek from Los Angeles to Lee Vining, a distance of two hundred and seventy-five miles. In those days, just making this trip could be a real adventure. It was all two-lane roads with a speed limit of fifty-five miles per hour—a snail's pace compared to driving the road today.

After reaching Lee Vining, it was five miles of twisty, steep, and rocky dirt road to reach the Log Cabin Mine. This was the first indication that the comforts and conveniences of city life were left far behind.

The first business at hand for my father was to find a location near the mine to set up his family's new home. The beautiful meadow south of the main mine buildings was the ideal spot and was where my father, my mother, and I spent our first summer at the mine. This area is known as the Simpson Meadow.

Our first home at the mine was hand-built by my grandfather, Dave Keith, my mother's father. He was an accomplished carpenter and had constructed a tent for us to take from Los Angeles. He made this custom tent complete with a wooden foundation and ensured that his daughter and grandson would have all the "modern" conveniences that tent living could provide.

Grandpa Dave with his tent, circa 1940. (Cassidy Family Archives)

My mother, being a sophisticated graduate of Hollywood High School, did not have the background or training to prepare her to deal with outdoor living. Outhouses and wild animals were definitely not on the curriculum at Hollywood High. I can only imagine the fear she felt as she was forced to ward off the bears and mountain lions that would prowl around her tent at night while she was alone with her baby, her husband away running the mine.

Frank Sr. and Carol Cassidy in front of their tent in Simpson Meadow, circa 1940 (note the outhouse). (Cassidy Family Archives)

But my mother learned quickly. When she heard the noises of the prowling animals around the tent at night, she would arm herself with a .22 rifle. She would guard the tent and her baby with that rile held across her knees. One night, my father made a surprise trip down from the mine to the tent. Imagine his surprise when he opened the tent flap door and came face-to-face with a .22 rifle in the hands of his young bride. Fortunately, she did not pull the trigger, and we made it through the summer without any bullet wounds.

Through that summer of 1940, my mother cared for me, now two years old, in her tent home in Simpson Meadow while my father ran the Log Cabin Mine. She would take me on her daily trips by truck to go the one-mile distance on dirt roads to the mine office. She took care of all the mine business, including typing reports, keeping the books, and acting as the paymaster, and attended to my needs as an infant at the same time. It was clear that my father needed my mother as his partner in order to adequately perform his superintendent's duties.

Breakfast at the tent, circa 1940. (Cassidy Family Archives)

Boy's best friend at the tent, circa 1940. (Cassidy Family Archives)

With winter approaching, my parents knew that a high-country gold mine with harsh winter snows was not the place for a baby. But my father needed my mother to continue managing the business side of the mine operation. My parents agonized over the dilemma of how to keep me safe while running the mine through the winter ahead.

In the late fall of 1940, we made the trip down the mountain back to Los Angeles for a business meeting with Mr. Garbutt and included a visit to my Grandma and Grandpa Cassidy. My parents made the decision that it was best to leave me with my grandparents in the city for the winter. To be successful, the Log Cabin Mine needed both my mother and father, but it would not be safe for me to be at the mine during the winter months. This was an extremely difficult decision for my parents, and my mother spoke many times during the years of the extreme suffering of leaving her baby.

Grandpa Jim Cassidy, "Pop-Pop," and me. (Cassidy Family Archives)

Once the hard decision was made to ensure my welfare, my parents faced their next challenge of preparing for the approaching winter at ten thousand feet. My mom would tell the story of being packed to the gills with supplies and provisions in the truck for the trip to the mine. To deal with the isolation and being the only woman amongst all the miners (she was never worried about her safety with my father as her protector), she packed newspapers, books, magazines, and, of course, snowshoes to occupy her time.

Besides managing mine business during the winter of 1940–41, my tall, sophisticated mother became an accomplished snowshoer. To survive the freezing temperatures, she traded the tent in Simpson Meadow for the superintendent's cabin. Despite not having her young son, she was comforted by having a few upgrades, including running water and an indoor bathroom. She enjoyed keeping house and found pleasure in her peek at Mono Lake from the front porch. The cabin was about two hundred yards from the mine office, allowing her to perfect her snowshoeing skills on trips back and forth from the mine to the cabin in order to attend to mine business.

My father, with my mom as his helpmate, managed the Log Cabin Mine through the winter, and despite the significant sacrifices, it was a success.

Frank Sr. in front of the cook shack, circa 1940. (Cassidy Family Archives)

Man of the mountains, circa 1940. No wonder he fought
Mickey Walker! (Cassidy Family Archives)

Life in Lee Vining: The Early Years

In the spring of 1941, my parents made the trip from the Log Cabin Mine to Los Angeles to take me, now three years old, with them back to the mine. Having coped with this difficult separation from her baby, my mother made it clear that she wanted something more for her son than the canvas walls of the tent in Simpson Meadow where we lived the previous summer. My father quickly agreed—it reduced the risk of him walking into the muzzle of a .22 rifle again! In the summer of 1941, they decided that the family would divide time between the superintendent's cabin at the mine in the summer and a rented house in Lee Vining during the winter.

Me at the steps of the superintendent's cabin, circa 1941–42. (Cassidy Family Archives)

Me at the mine, circa 1941–42. (Cassidy Family Archives)

Our house in Lee Vining was very close to the house owned by the Blaver family. Their son, Harry Jr., and I were close in age. One of my early memories is my mother and Elma Blaver beating sticks together by the ditch that ran between the two houses to ward off rattlesnakes to enable Harry Jr. and me to safely play our favorite game of cowboys and Indians. I was always the cowboy who was shot by Harry's arrows. Harry and I were good friends for many years, and I have the fondest memories of him.

My mother and Elma Blaver also became very good friends. The men were too busy at the mine or running local businesses to form and lead a Cub Scout pack, so in later years, my mother and Elma obtained a special approval from the Los Angeles Boy Scouts to establish the Lee Vining Cub Scouts. At that time, they were the only female Cub Scout leaders in the state.

The Lee Vining Cub Scouts at Mono Lake, circa 1947. Left to right: John Murphy, Don Murphy, Nick Cassidy (me), Ron Donnelly, Donnie Hess, Alan Blaver, Harry Blaver Jr., Dick Miller. (Cassidy Family Archives)

Augie Hess (right) and Harry Blaver Sr. (Elma's husband and owner of the Lee Vining Market). My dad had invited them for a visit to the mine (circa 1950s), and Augie is dressed in his old outfit when he worked in the mine as a mucker. (Courtesy of Vineca Hess)

The schools in Lee Vining were small; grades one through four were in one room and five through eight in another. In 1946, I was enrolled in Lee Vining Grammar School. One of my first teachers was Nora Archer, who was nearing the end of her teaching career. Mrs. Archer was the first superintendent of schools in Mono County, and I feel that I was very fortunate to have had her as a teacher.

Every morning started the same way. First we stood and saluted the flag, and then we would listen to "Cool Water" by the Sons of the Pioneers, apparently one of Mrs. Archer's favorites. Mrs. Archer was no-nonsense. If you were not performing your work, she would sneak up on you and rap your knuckles with a yardstick. (No, she never got sued.) These were consistent routines and tough lessons, but looking back, I'm damn glad every morning started that way—it was the best preparation for my later years in the U.S. Air Force!

Mining and Milling

In the early forties, my father continued to manage the Log Cabin Mine. This included transporting men and supplies to the mine by truck in the summer and by snowshoes (later a Sno-Cat) in the winter. There were no food refrigerators at the mine, and the supplies that needed to remain cold were placed in the meat house, which was one of the original structures at the mine. The walls consisted of logs that had to be six to eight feet in diameter. This provided good insulation for the food that had to be kept at lower temperatures. The miners lived in the bunkhouse, and the cooks lived in the large cook shack. The cook shack was also the mess hall where the miners ate their meals.

The Meat House. (Cassidy Family Archives)

31

My father had increased the insulation of the meat house by placing pine needles between the logs, which was a very ingenious idea. Later on in the fifties, I remember watching my dad construct a large freezer complete with 220 wiring within the original meat house. The miners no longer had to depend on large logs and pine needles to refrigerate the necessary food.

The mining process and extraction of gold is a technical art. In this particular hard-rock mining, the gold was usually imbedded in quartz rock or ore. My father's expertise in geology and extensive exploration and prospecting on the surface gave him a good idea where to look for the quartz ore, or veins, underground.

The mining operations started by removing the ore from the mine. The miners would go down into the mineshaft and drill holes in the rock containing the ore using jackhammers powered by compressed air that was generated above ground by the Ingersoll Rand air compressor located in the hoist house. They would then load the holes with blasting powder and set the caps and fuses, giving them just enough time to safely exit the mine.

Miner drilling for a round of dynamite. (Cassidy Family Archives)

To exit the mine, they would then ride to the surface on the skip, a cage that lifts and lowers men and equipment in the mine shaft. A large cable was attached to the top of the skip and ran three hundred to four hundred feet to the surface and to the top of the gallis frame, where it wrapped around the wheel and was pulled down to the hoist house. The cable would wrap on the large drum that was powered by a large electric motor and controlled by the hoist operator.

The hoist house. (Cassidy Family Archives)

Hoist control levers (brake and clutch) and the operator's chair. (Cassidy Family Archives)

After the blast, the men, usually accompanied by my father, would descend back into the mine. My father would have on his hard hat with light along with his prospector's pick. With his expertise, it did not take him long to decide which quartz ore was to be processed for gold and which rock was not gold-bearing. This non-gold- bearing rock had to be removed after the blast in order to reach the quartz ore. The rock that did not qualify for processing was termed "overburden."

The men who had set and triggered the blasts were classified as miners, and the men who shoveled the ore after the blasts were called muckers. The ore was mucked into ore cars that were on rails leading to the bottom of the shaft and onto the skip. The miners would then signal up to the hoist operator by pulling on the bell cable. The series of bell rings would designate which cars were overburden and which cars were to be processed for gold.

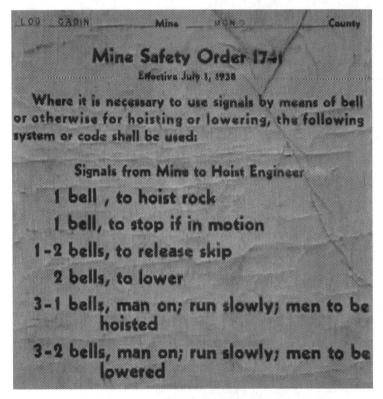

Actual sign from the Log Cabin Mine showing the bell signals.
(Courtesy the movie *Log Cabin Mine, From Mine to Mint*)

The mine had four levels, with the bottom level also serving as the drain tunnel, because water would accumulate at the lower levels and had to have a way out of the mine. The drain tunnel was approximately fifteen hundred feet long and opened up to the surface lower down in Tioga Canyon.

One of the miners who worked for my father (circa 1940) was Elmer (Buddy) Bayer Sr. His son, Buddy, and I later became neighbors in Lee Vining. It seems that Buddy Sr. was working at the fourth level and had a new helper who was called the rookie. One day during a break, they heard a creaking noise (probably just shifting timbers). Buddy thought he could scare the rookie by telling him that it was the Tommyknockers and that it meant imminent danger. This joking did scare the rookie, but it turned out to be a premonition. The following day, a cave-in occurred at the exact spot where they had been the previous day. The cave-in buried the machinery and drilling equipment and could have killed any miner close by. From then on, the rookie firmly believed in Tommyknockers, and I think Buddy might have also given them more serious consideration.

Elmer "Buddy" Bayer Sr. working at the third level of the Log Cabin Mine in June of 1940. (Courtesy of Elmer Bayer Jr and Lily Mathieu)

During the mining process, the overburden was hoisted to the surface and the ore car was then pushed on rails to one of the two designated dumps.

Ore cars on the rails leading to one of the overburden
dumps. (Cassidy Family Archives)

The ore to be processed for gold would be hoisted up past the surface, where
it was pushed by rail to the first of two bins, which contained a rock crusher at
the bottom. The rock crusher was used to crush the rock to a smaller size.

View of the covered rail path leading to the first bin
and the bin itself. (Cassidy Family Archives)

The first rock crusher. (Courtesy of MBHS)

After the initial rock crushing, the ore traveled upward on a long conveyor belt and was deposited in a second bin. This second bin also had a rock crusher at the bottom that further reduced the size of the ore.

This conveyor belt was probably about fifty yards long and fairly steep. There was a wooden ramp to the side of the conveyor belt that was used to access the belt. (This ramp served double duty as the perfect challenge for young daredevils. I vividly remember as a young boy running up and down the conveyor belt ramp. It was a thrill to challenge the rules and attempt to defy gravity, but to this day I consider myself lucky that my mother did not know of my ramp exploits!)

The conveyor that I used to love to run up and down—if
I didn't get caught. (Cassidy Family Archives)

The second storage bin with the second rock crusher below. (Mt.
Warren is in the background.) (Cassidy Family Archives)

The second rock-crusher (inside view). Notice the crushed ore spilling out to the short conveyor belt. (Courtesy of MBHS)

The ore then went up a shorter conveyor belt and into the ball mill. The mill was a huge rotating drum that contained approximately 750 steel balls (similar to those used in shot-putting).

The short conveyor belt to the ball mill. (Courtesy of MBHS)

The ball mill. (Courtesy of MBHS)

A sample of the balls contained in the ball mill on display at the
Old School House Museum. (Cassidy Family Archives)

The mill would run continuously for a period of time. Water was added to the rotating drum, and the ore would be reduced to slurry. The slurry containing the gold was poured over a series of amalgamating plates coated with quicksilver (mercury). The gold, being heavier than the remaining rock, would sink to the bottom and actually combine with the mercury, forming a compound called amalgam (hence amalgamating plates).

The mill would be shut down, and the amalgam was scraped from the plates and formed into a thick ball. The ball would be placed into a metal urn (or retort) and heated to a certain temperature over a period of time. The mercury would boil off to be recovered, leaving the proverbial pot of gold.

Scraping the plates. It is possible this is Frank Garbutt himself. (Courtesy of MBHS)

The pot of gold, with tongs and the urn. (Courtesy of MBHS)

Transporting the pot of gold was an adventure in itself. My father would box and seal the gold per U.S. Bureau of Mines regulations. He would then drive down the rugged mine road towards Lee Vining, his trusty .38 revolver by his side. Armed guards also accompanied him. Upon arriving in town, my father would meet the Lee Vining postmaster and deposit the gold at the U.S. Post Office, which was at that time part of the Lee Vining Market. These meetings were always arranged in advance, and the days and times were always varied to outwit any robbery attempts. This careful planning ensured that each gold shipment was delivered from Lee Vining to the final destination: the U.S. Mint.

Mining During Winter

The mining and milling process was performed year-round, but with the winter months came a new difficulty: snow levels up to twenty-five feet deep! On weekends, my father, with some of the men, would snowshoe down the mine road to Highway 120, a five-mile journey. From there, they would travel to Lee Vining in trucks with chains on all four wheels. Some of the men preferred to stay at the mine, where they lived in the bunkhouse and ate in the cook shack.

A winter scene of the Log Cabin Mine. (Cassidy Family Archives)

The Log Cabin Mine bunkhouses in winter. (Cassidy Family Archives)

Looking out the cook-shack door in winter at the steps
carved in the snow. (Cassidy Family Archives)

Coming to town with chains on all four wheels. (Courtesy of MBHS)

The married men would visit with their families in the local towns over the weekend. Many of the single men emptied their paychecks at one of the saloons in Lee Vining (either Bodie Mike's or Julio's, previously located where Nicely's Restaurant is today) and then danced to the Hess Orchestra in Hess Hall (currently the Mono Lake Committee building). I can remember as a youngster sitting on the row of benches in the hall while my parents danced. I witnessed the Hess Orchestra in action and can still picture Gus on the French horn. What fun!

This was the actual Hess Hall; this is now the Mono Lake Committee Building. (Courtesy of MBHS)

But after the fun of the weekend, my father had the task of gathering all the men and supplies that would be transported by snowshoe back to the mine on Monday. At times, gathering the men proved more challenging than collecting the supplies. I remember one story where my father had to travel to Reno, Nevada, to retrieve one of the cooks. The cook did not return to work, and my father was forced to make the six-hour trek to roust him out of one of the many opium dens in Reno at the time. Monitoring the cooks was an unwritten part of the superintendent's job description.

The cooks at the mine were really a separate society, which posed different managerial challenges for my father. This sometimes meant intervening in disputes where the weapons of choice were usually cleavers. My father settled these disputes peaceably, but he was a formidable man when necessary.

During the winter, the snowshoe trip from the mine to Lee Vining presented other challenges. The trek was long, arduous, and freezing cold. From the time I was a young boy, I can remember my father appearing at the front door in our house in Lee Vining, hardly visible under his parka and covered with icicles after the long, frosty trip. But my mother, always my father's helpmate, would provide the perfect solution: a hot shower and a cold martini! I can remember the steam from the shower flowing out of the bathroom as my mother handed in his martini. My mother always said it was the best way to warm up after a long snowshoe trip. I never once heard my father disagree.

Dad's snowshoes. (Cassidy Family Archives)

The trip up to the mine in the winter was no picnic, either. Many times, meat had to be transported to the mine from Lee Vining using only backpacks and snowshoes. On one such trip, a miner, Pete Archer (the son of my elementary school teacher, Mrs. Archer), had snowshoed down and picked up fresh meat from Harry Blaver at the Lee Vining Market. While snowshoeing back to the mine, Pete heard a low growl some yards behind him. A hungry mountain lion was pursuing Pete's backpack or even Pete himself. Pete, hoping it was the backpack, would toss a piece of meat to distract the approaching lion. This went on for at least two miles in the snow, up the hill on the way to the mine. When Pete arrived at the mine, the backpack was empty, but Pete was alive.

Later that night, my father and Pete Mathieu, who was my father's foreman for many years, left the mine on snowshoes to track the lion and verified every detail of the horrific event. Later, when I heard this story, I knew fear caused by this event was the source of Pete Archer's very light complexion.

Supplies being transported to the mine in winter (Pete Mathieu and Mike the Dog). (Cassidy Family Archives)

The War Years

In 1942, President Roosevelt signed Executive Order Number 208, banning the mining of non-strategic material during World War II. This order effectively shut down gold mining and converted all mining operations to extract lead, zinc, and silver for strategic purposes.

As a result, Mr. Garbutt reassigned my father to be the general superintendent of his lead and zinc mine, known as the Tennessee Schuylkill Mine, in Chloride, Arizona. This assignment lasted about five years, and my mother and I accompanied my father.

Dad and I in Chloride, circa 1943. (Cassidy Family Archives)

Even at six years old, I was awed by the extent of the buildings and structures (such as the gallis frames) at the mine.

The Tennessee Schuylkill Mine, with Chloride, Arizona, in the background, circa 1943. (Cassidy Family Archives)

The government had close association with this operation, and I can remember many army trucks and Jeeps with uniformed men inspecting the mine.

Dad with the army at the Tennessee Schuylkill. (Cassidy Family Archives)

During this time period, we made several trips to visit family in Santa Monica, California, which required crossing the Hoover Dam. I can remember being escorted in convoys of approximately twenty cars across the top of Hoover Dam. An army jeep with a .50 caliber machine gun traveled at the rear of the convoy to prevent any sabotage of the dam.

During this time, there was constant fear that the Japanese would cross the Pacific Ocean and bomb the coast. Blackouts, where it was illegal to have any form of light, were frequent. I remember numerous occasions of riding in the backseat of the family car at night as a blackout was ordered. Boy, it was dark! My father would maneuver the car by feeling the way down Santa Monica Blvd. to Fourth Street on our way to my grandmother's house.

During this time, food rationing was also in effect. This included sugar. I can remember my beloved grandfather, Pop-Pop, sneaking his sugar ration to me for my breakfast cereal.

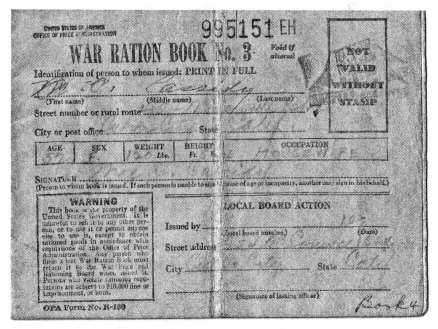

World War II ration stamp book. (Cassidy Family Archives)

When I remember the years at the Tennessee Schuylkill Mine, my respect for my father is immense. Imagine being general manager of one of the most critical mines during World War II, responsible for up to one hundred people mining, processing, and transporting lead and zinc necessary to support the war effort. It was a challenging time, and my father's success was a direct result of his strong drive, dedication, and perseverance.

Frank C. Cassidy, General Manager,
Tennessee Mine & Mill, Chloride, Arizona

A lot of responsibility. (Cassidy Family Archives)

Back to Gold Mining

When the executive order against non-war-related mining was lifted in 1946, Mr. Garbutt sent my father back to the Log Cabin Mine to resume his duties as general superintendent. My father was anxious to return to the Log Cabin Mine and to continue extracting the gold he knew was there. By this time, the Log Cabin Mine consisted of seventy-two patented claims, which covered a lot of territory, approximately eighty-one acres.

My father continued full-time gold mining and processing at the Log Cabin Mine until 1948. During this time, my mom, dad, and I lived in the superintendent's cabin in the summer and in Lee Vining during the fierce winter months.

I was very fortunate as a youngster to be able to watch the full-time operation of the mine, which occurred from 1946–48. Even though I was the only youngster at the mine, it was not a lonely existence. The day-to-day workings of a fully operational gold mine always had my complete attention.

Frank Sr. and his family were elated to return to the Log Cabin Mine

The Price of Gold Only Maintains Operations

In 1948, it was obvious that the times had changed and the focus of the operations had to adjust accordingly.

In 1933, President Franklyn Roosevelt had signed Executive Order Number 6102, which forbade the hoarding of gold and forced private sale of gold to the federal government. This paved the way for the Gold Reserve Act of 1934, which set the price of gold at thirty-five dollars per ounce, and it did not change until 1971.

As a result of this fixed price, the overhead costs of operating the mine gradually increased and the expenses outweighed the profits. As a result, the gold tonnage produced at the mine gradually reduced from 1946–48. In 1948, with the price of gold remaining at thirty-five dollars per ounce, it was no longer profitable to actively mine at the Log Cabin Mine.

Starting in 1948, my father focused his efforts on maintenance tasks at the Log Cabin Mine. The goal was to be prepared to start active processing should the price per ounce increase. The mine was kept in complete readiness. If the price of gold rose to an appreciable level, the mine could be fully operational in a very short time.

My father had also hoped to construct a cyanide plant at the mine. The slurry that was left after the extraction of gold still had a concentration of mercury, and it was pumped to the top of the hill in a large pipe by a series of pumps protected by pump houses. These houses are still visible today.

One of the pump houses in winter. (Cassidy Family Archives)

The slurry was deposited in a series of tailings ponds at the top of the hill. This was done to avoid the slurry going down Tioga Canyon and contaminating Mono Lake.

One of the tailings ponds. Lee Vining Peak is in the background. (Cassidy Family Archives)

The cyanide plant would reclaim a high percentage of the gold left in the slurry (up to 98 percent) and eliminate the mercury.

Again, due to the static price of gold, the cost prevented the construction of the plant. Gus and Bill Hess had hauled sections of the plant up the hill. These sections are still there today.

Parts of the cyanide plant (never constructed). (Cassidy Family Archives)

Maintenance activities included operation above ground and below ground.

Maintenance Operations Underground

Constant inspection of the underground tunnels, or drifts, were conducted to look for occasional cave-ins, which were caused by decaying timber. Any decayed timber would have to be replaced in order to keep the tunnels open. This ensured the physical safety and mental stability of the miners. Miners were understandably very superstitious people. The Tommyknockers were only one example.

Lumber was needed for this maintenance process. A lumber set consisted of four posts or sections of tree trunks. These posts were made from trees that had been cut down previously on the expansive mine property. They were then put through the framing shed, which contained a large rotating saw. The singing sound that the saw made as it was sectioning the trees could be heard for miles around.

The framing shed. (Cassidy Family Archives)

The housing for the singing saw (the blade has
been stolen). (Cassidy Family Archives)

The framing shed was approximately fifty yards down a slope to the mineshaft. I remember a miner, Joe Saulque, carrying a post on each shoulder from the framing shed down to the mine shaft and into the skip. The posts were between six to eight feet in length. Joe was a very powerful man, as miners usually were.

Posts that were to be used in the mine, in front of the framing shed. (Cassidy Family Archives)

The trail Joe Salque used in winter. (Cassidy Family Archives)

The posts, along with two-by-twelve lumber, were then lowered on the skip to the level at which the cave-in had occurred. The material (rock, shale, etc.) from the cave-in had been previously mucked into the ore cars and transported by the skip to the surface and to the dumps.

The posts were placed one on each side of the drift, approximately ten feet apart. The two-by-twelve lumber was then positioned on the top and the sides to connect the posts. In this way, about a ten-foot section of drift could be replaced. The process usually occurred in the winter but occasionally in the summer. The men and material were lowered and raised in the shaft on the skip. The hoist operator that handled this job was usually Clarence Miller. The men working in the mine wore heavy coats, rubber boots, and a battery pack that was connected to a light on their miner's hard hat. It was dark, wet, and cold down in the mine.

Dad and two miners ready to go to work (circa 1941). (Cassidy Family Archives)

Maintenance Operations
Above Ground

My father was very protective over the mine property and structures. Maintaining the above-ground operation included structure repairs and preventing trespassers. I would often help Pete Mathieu walk the perimeter of the property every fall to replace any damaged No Trespassing signs. It was a long hike.

No Trespassing was a specific warning for deer hunters. (My father was hell on deer hunters.) A vehicle patrol occurred three times per day during deer season, and my father was diligent about this task.

Of course, chasing deer hunters was a small part of the above-ground maintenance. All the buildings and structures had to be kept in good order. The electrical equipment was maintained in top working condition. Air compressors, air hoses, and mining tools ranging from picks and shovels to jackhammers were constantly inspected. One can only imagine the range of activities necessary to keep a functional gold mine ready for full operation.

My father, as superintendent, ensured these below- and above-ground maintenance activities from 1948 to 1968—twenty years!

An example of the above-ground buildings and machinery that
had to be kept in readiness. (Cassidy Family Archives)

Life in Lee Vining: The Later Years

While my father focused on maintaining the mine, my family—which now included my baby sister, Kathleen—began living in Lee Vining year-round in 1950.

Our first house was a rental whose front had been a dry goods store. My mother converted this part of the house into the mine office. Our house and two others occupied the space that is now Nicely's parking lot. (Nicely's Restaurant occupies the space that was formerly Julio's Saloon and the Sez Bill Café.)

There was one larger house close to ours, where Bill and Clara Fuller lived. Bill and Clara owned the Sez Bill Café. The Pete Mathieu family later occupied the third house.

Even our first house had a link to mining history. My father told me the story about a miner who had become drunk and shot himself in the bathtub prior to our renting the house. Everyone assumed it was accidental, but I disliked the bathtub from that time on.

In that house, my bedroom window faced the side entrance of Julio's Saloon, a popular spot for miners, locals, marines from the Pickel Meadow's Cold Weather Training Facility, and sheep-men. In the warm summer nights, I would lie in bed with the window open and wait for a distinctive sound. One of the sheep-men, Amelio Carbaga, would emit a loud yell-howl from the saloon that lasted for at least ten seconds. This howl was familiar to most residents of Lee Vining, and Amelio only did this yell when he was at a certain point of happiness in the saloon. That is a fun memory for me.

Starting in 1952 through 1955, I attended Lee Vining High School. Similar to elementary school, there were only five students in my graduating class. Harry Jr. and I attended Lee Vining High School together. Our after-school sports programs included baseball in the spring, football in the fall, and skiing in the winter.

Football at Lee Vining High involved the entire town. We had two of the best coaches possible: C. Gerald Hasty, the principal of Lee Vining High School, and Hugh Deaton, a teacher and former varsity basketball star at the University of Virginia. The team and town were fortunate to have both men as coaches and mentors.

Harry and I filled two spots on the six–man (later eight-man) football team. Harry Jr. was the quarterback. Our football field was a beautiful meadow in Lee Vining Canyon. Goal posts had been erected specifically for us. On game days, the whole town would participate. The field would be surrounded by cheering fans and honking cars. Life in a small town was great!

Our team played in the league that included Coleville, Big Pine, Bishop, and Smith Valley, Nevada. Those farm boys were big and tough! We did manage to beat the Bishop Junior Varsity team one year, 58–6. This was quite an accomplishment because Bishop was the big city compared to Lee Vining.

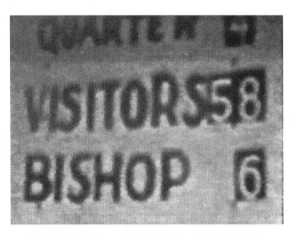

Scoreboard from Bishop Union High School
football field (Cassidy Family Archives)

During the winter, when football season was over, skiing was the focus. Don Banta, with the help of others, including the ski team, had constructed a series of three rope tows up the mountain behind Lee Vining. The poles which held the pulleys for the ropes had to be set in cement. The crew could not dig the hole for the top pole because the ground was solid rock. Don Banta enlisted the aid of George Totlin, a local miner, to get the hole dug. Many of those poles, including the one at the top, are still visible today.

Our physical education class took place on the Lee Vining slopes. We were released from school at two fifteen and skied from three fifteen until dark every day. We enjoyed the rush of the downhill speed and didn't mind the freezing cold—until the walk home! During the thirty-minute trek to our house, my feet would begin to thaw—a painful process, but worth the time on the slopes.

Our Lee Vining High School ski team, coached by Don Banta, was highly successful. We won the Sierra Nevada Interscholastic Ski Federation Championship three years in a row in the early fifties. One of the championship races was held on the Lee Vining hill, and Don was always proud that we could beat them on their hill or ours. We competed against teams from Tahoe-Truckee, California, and Reno, Nevada, and even against teams from as far away as Big Bear, California. That trophy still sits proudly in the Lee Vining High School trophy case.

Part of the championship Lee Vining High School ski team with coach Don Banta and Principal C. Gerald Hasty. (Courtesy of MBHS)

But even as an accomplished skier, I was no match for the men at the mine, especially my father and Pete Mathieu. As a teenager in the early fifties, I jumped at the chance to accompany my father and Pete Mathieu on a winter trip to the mine. They were on snowshoes, and I had my skis.

They could navigate the hills straight ahead on their snowshoes, and I had to side-step with the skis. My father and Pete passed me up; not a good thing for a teenage ego. I was able to somewhat redeem myself when we got to the top of the hill since it was downhill to the mine from there. I almost caught up to them, but I was one tired and humbled skier.

Me on skis, circa 1951. (Cassidy Family Archives)

I gained immense respect for my dad, Pete, the other miners, and my mom as they spent many winters snowshoeing to, from, and around the mine.

Working at the Log Cabin Mine

From 1948 until 1952, when I started high school, I was able to help my father and his crew at the mine during the summers while they performed their maintenance operations. My father also conducted the exploratory work to find the gold veins, assayed the material, and coordinated all processing. I observed and was able to help with many of the tasks. I remember being allowed to proudly hold the ends of the picks and shovels while my father sharpened their metal points in the forge, which was located in the mine shop.

One process that I observed was diamond drilling. Lengths of pipe (about one-inch diameter) were drilled deep into the ground. The first length included a diamond bit to drill through the rock. The diamond drill setup reminded me of a mini oil rig. My father examined the cores of ore retrieved from the pipe. This aided him in mapping the various gold veins.

My father was also responsible for many of the complex aspects of mining, such as assaying of gold. The assay office was a small building just behind the hoist house. My father frequently did assaying of ore samples for gold content. This process took about six hours and involved heating crucibles that contained the material to be assayed in a small furnace until they were red hot. After the crucibles cooled, the materials were treated with various chemicals and transferred to very delicate scales. I actually got to help my father during this six-hour process (which seemed like an eternity to a teenage boy).

The assay house with the compressed air tank and
Mt. Warren. (Cassidy Family Archives)

I realized years later when taking several chemistry courses as a student at the University of California, Berkeley, how knowledgeable my father had to have been to accurately analyze the gold content in various ore samples from different sites. The process was complicated, but my father was a true master.

During my time at the mine, I also helped Pete Mathieu with above-ground maintenance, such as repairing buildings, replacing the No Trespassing signs, etc. I really enjoyed the annual trip around the property. We would pack our lunch and plenty of water. The trek was long, but what beautiful scenery.

Just a portion of the mine property that Pete Mathieu and
I walked every fall. (Cassidy Family Archives)

When I started high school in 1952, I alternated between my role at the mine and summer jobs in Lee Vining. I worked as a dishwasher for Bill Faulkner in his restaurant. (This was before the introduction of automated washing units and posed a physical challenge for a tall young man at a low sink!) I continued washing dishes for Betty Kellogg, who took over the restaurant and renamed it the Kellogg's Café. Later, I obtained a position as a service station attendant for Vincent Kellogg at his Richfield station and then at the Union 76 on Highway 395 in the center of town.

In my spare time during high school, I still enjoyed helping my father at the mine with the various summer maintenance tasks.

During my college years, 1955–59, at the University of California, Berkeley, I worked during the summers for my father at the Log Cabin Mine. I was the superintendent's son, but he spared no mercy. I was expected to do my share of the physical labor. Each summer, it would take at least two weeks to rebuild my tough miner's physique. My parents would make the long trek to Berkeley to bring me home for the summer. My mother would look at me and say that I looked exhausted after studying so long and hard on final exams, but my father would say that it was time to go to work! I can still remember stepping onto that skip to be lowered four hundred feet down into the mine. It was none too steady, and it jiggled. It was a good thing Pete Mathieu was usually along to calm my nerves. Pete was my father's foreman for many years, and a finer man I never met.

Pete Mathieu doing some winter maintenance (note the
Camel cigarette). (Cassidy Family Archives)

During those summers, I worked as a mucker and would help Pete
Mathieu load one ore car after another at the various levels of the mine.

I also worked above ground at the Lake View operation. This was so-
named because of its precarious perch on the mountainside, about four
hundred feet below the top of the hill. My father built the road down to the
Lake View, which consisted of a series of switchbacks. The Blue Beetle, an old
army four-by-four truck that my father purchased and painted a bright blue,
would inch its way up and down this road to the Lake View.

The Blue Beetle, along with the other Chevy truck. (Cassidy Family Archives)

Flat-landers taken on this trip were known to wet their pants out of fear. One missed maneuver on the Lake View road would end with a swim in Mono Lake some three thousand feet below!

At the Lake View, my father had sunk a seventy-five-foot incline shaft. He knew that there was a gold vein there due to his geological experience and information gained from the diamond-drilling operations. The Lake View operations were also kept ready for full-time processing should the price of gold rise. During the summers, I was the hoist operator for this operation. It was my job to run the hoist, which contained the ore, up the rails in the shaft and dump the contents in the dump area. The ore obtained would be transported by truck to the main mine and ball mill for processing.

On one occasion, my father told me, "Whatever you do, don't dump this load in the regular dump." Instead, I deposited it in another area, and my father covered it with a tarp. That single load was later processed and found to be worth a lot of money ... even by today's standards!

During my summers working there, I was constantly treated to the view of the mighty Sierras and the Mono Basin below. How much better can it get?

Memorable Adventures

Hard work at the Log Cabin Mine was a tough job, but we did have numerous memorable adventures.

As a teenager, I wanted to learn to water ski on Mono Lake. To make this possible, my father bought a small boat that we repaired and painted. He also purchased a twenty-five-horsepower Johnson outboard motor that he juiced up by milling the heads.

Frank Sr. with his first boat on Mono Lake, circa 1953. (Cassidy Family Archives)

My waterskiing experiences began with this boat, but my father decided that a bigger, better boat was needed. But just buying a bigger boat was too simple.

Instead, my father purchased books on boat building. He then commenced to build our own boat. This construction was done on the bottom floor of the mine bunkhouse in my father's spare time. I still do not know how he got that boat out of the bunkhouse. We can definitely add sea captain and boat builder to his long list of talents! I did learn to water ski and have many fond memories of my father captaining that blue and white boat.

The boat that Dad built (with daughter Kathleen alongside). (Cassidy Family Archives)

What fun it was to ski on Mono Lake. (Cassidy Family Archives)

My father was also an avid deer hunter, and each season provided new adventures. He was really tough on anyone who would violate the No Trespassing signs and attempt to hunt near the mine. I remember one night before the season opener when I was a little kid, my father and Pete Mathieu took me along on the ride to evict twelve drunken hunters camped in Simpson Meadow. As you can imagine, this was not a real safe task (Dad made sure I stayed in the truck). However, my father, with his trusty .38 and Pete, a former Mono County deputy sheriff, got the job done. The hunters were not too happy, but they left the mine property in search of other hunting areas.

My father and Pete would also use binoculars to scan the area looking for any wayward deer hunters. I can remember my father taking me along on a quick hike to firmly order some disobedient hunters off the mine property. My father was a deer hunter himself, and he usually had his buck within ten minutes of deer season opening, but I think he enjoyed hunting the hunters as much as or more than hunting deer.

Dad always got his buck (1946). (Cassidy Family Archives)

My father and Pete would travel the mine road daily by truck in the summer months. During deer season in the fall, they would carry my father's trusty 30-40 Craig rifle between them on the seat in case Pete Mathieu had not yet gotten his deer for the season. On one such trip, they spied a very large, six-point buck. Pete was going to bag the buck from the passenger seat window but was stricken with buck fever, not an uncommon disease during that time of year. Pete managed to eject all the shells from the 30-40 Craig without firing a single shot, and the buck proudly went into the woods. Pete got his deer soon after that, but the story of Pete and buck fever was retold for many years.

Unbeknownst to me, my sons had my father's 30-40 Craig (model 1899) beautifully restored, and they presented it to me on my seventieth birthday. The rifle and the memories connected with it will proudly remain in our family for years to come.

My father and Pete were also avid duck hunters. At that time, duck hunting was allowed on Mono Lake. One winter's day when I was about ten years old, they took me hunting with them. I was very excited to go along. They spotted some big mallards on the shore of Thompson Ranch, now the location of Mono Lake Park. We hunkered down in the creek bed leading to the lake. It was dry except for the snow on the ground.

When the mallards flew, my father and Pete knocked down four or five of them, but they landed out in the freezing cold water of Mono Lake. Drat! They did not have a retriever dog! At least I did not think they did. It was then I realized why they took me along. I became a Labrador retriever that day and did well in my new role, but I was one cold and shivering boy dressed down to his skivvies by the time we got back to the truck. They wrapped me in blankets and hurriedly drove me home to Lee Vining along with my collection of ducks.

Now, I never saw my mother get angry very often, but this time took first prize. If she had had a broom handy she would have taken it to my father and Pete. She hollered, "How dare you send my son to fetch ducks on Mono Lake in the winter!" My father somehow escaped her wrath and found a solution to warm my shivering body. The answer was my initiation to hard liquor: a B&B, or bourbon and Benedictine. This stiff spirit and a warm bath did the trick, and I was warm and relaxed by dinner. The roast duck we had for supper that night was well earned and delicious!

I have told this story to my family many times with my mother present, and she never failed to disappoint me with her response. She would stiffen her back, her blue eyes would begin to blaze, and she would say to her grandchildren, "Can you imagine using my son for a duck dog?" They loved it. In fact, when one of my sons downed his first mallard in the middle of a wild rose thicket on the shores of the Owens River, I again became a retriever and invaded the rose thicket to retrieve the duck. I had a few bloody scratches from the adventure and saw my mother's blue eyes blaze once again.

Unforgettable Challenges

Life at the Log Cabin Mine and in Lee Vining provided numerous adventures, but living in remote areas with intense weather conditions supplied its share of challenges, too.

Just traveling to and from Los Angeles to the Log Cabin Mine was a challenge. We made this trip often to visit family. Crossing the Mojave Desert in the warm weather required planning and preparation. My dad always carried at least two of the old canvas water bags in case of a breakdown. On one trip, when I was eight years old, we broke down in the middle of the desert two miles short of Red Mountain on Highway 395. In this pre-cell phone era, there was no choice but to walk through the desolate desert to the closest town, all the while praying that a tow truck and mechanic were available. It was my father's preparedness and foresight that enabled him to handle any situation. And this was no exception. He had the supplies needed to make the walk to town and negotiate with the local garage to retrieve and repair the car. Thanks to good planning, we always avoided potentially dangerous situations!

When my sister, Kathleen, was born on May 19, 1949, in Southern California, my mother developed severe complications after delivery and had to remain in the hospital for an extended period. Since the mine needed his attention also, my father and I returned to the mine while my mother and baby sister stayed in the hospital in Southern California. My concerned and worried father made daily trips from the mine to Lee Vining in order to use the phone to check on my mother's condition. When my father learned that my mother had survived the emergency surgery and was in good condition, we were both overcome with relief. We were elated on our way back up to the mine and were thankful for our blessings.

Mom and daughter, Kathleen, safely back in Lee Vining, circa 1949–50. (Cassidy Family Archives)

Dad and me with baby Kath. (Cassidy Family Archives)

During our years in Lee Vining, we experienced some heavy winters. I remember having to cut the screen out of the top of the front door of our house in order to get outside after a heavy overnight snow while my father was at the mine. I was able to shovel the door clear so we could get to the Lee Vining Market for needed food and supplies. Even though it was a short distance, the deep snow made it a challenge. My mom's snowshoes were stored at the Log Cabin Mine, so she had to resort to boots. Of course, the boots were stylish ones, as she had not lost her sophistication even though she had definitely become a mountain lady.

The heavy snows could cause many problems. Highway 395 was a two-lane road back then (not the four-lane freeway that it is now). It was once closed for fourteen days. Needed supplies such as bread and milk for the community had to be air-dropped to us. The need was clear when local residents Roger and Gladys Kelly and Marge Gripper trampled "HELP" in the snow above Lee Vining.

The nearest physician was in Bridgeport, twenty-five miles away. Ida Cecil was a practical nurse and our only medical help in Lee Vining. Ida and Carl owned Cecil's Sporting Goods, now Bells. On one occasion, I had contracted some cyclic neck spasm condition. Fortunately, Ida was able to break the muscle spasms with a morphine injection.

Life at the Log Cabin Mine and in Lee Vining presented many challenges, most of which have now become fond memories, but the toughest challenge that still tears at my heart was the closing of the Log Cabin Mine.

Closing the Log Cabin Mine

The maintenance operation at the mine started in 1948 and continued to 1968. During this entire time, my father was responsible for ensuring that the mine would be ready for full-scale operation should the price of gold rise above thirty-five dollars per ounce and once again justify the mining operation.

I watched my father continue to hope for the price of gold to rise until his death in 1968. Sadly, it did not happen in his lifetime.

The nation lifted the gold standard on August 15, 1971. President Richard Nixon ended trading of gold at the fixed price of thirty-five dollars per ounce, and the price of gold began to steadily rise. As of this writing (Feb. 2010), the price of gold is one thousand one hundred and eighteen dollars per ounce.

Without my father, there was no one with the knowledge or expertise to continue to maintain the mine. Shortly after his death, the Hathaway-Garbutt families donated the mine to the Boy Scouts of America, Los Angeles Area Council.

The sign pointing out the mine road after the donation to
the Boy Scouts of America. (Cassidy Family Archives)

The Boy Scouts briefly leased the mine to some short-lived and unsuccessful companies trying to extract gold from the property. One such company was U.S. Tile from Corona, California, whose effort lasted only two years, ending in 1982.

The U.S. Forest Service acquired the mine, with the many veins of untapped gold, and the surrounding area, on February 20, 1991.

Preserving the History of the Log Cabin Mine

Beginning in the nineties, the U.S. Forest Service recognized the historical significance of the Log Cabin Mine and attempted to establish it as a historical site.

The thought of restoring the mine was very exciting to my family and me. I had recently semi-retired from veterinary surgery and was living in Bishop, California, roughly a seventy-five-minute drive to the Log Cabin Mine.

I discussed with Nancy Upham of the U.S. Forest Service the possibility of my acting as a docent in the summers by giving tours through the mine property. The Forest Service was very receptive to this idea, but the funding was not available for the project due to the cost of upgrading the surface of the mine to meet safety standards.

Without adequate funding, the mine buildings and structures continued to decay. Vandals also contributed to the deterioration of the site. Beginning in 2003, in an attempt to preserve the mine, a group of concerned local citizens from the Lee Vining area (many from the Mono Basin Historical Society) accompanied by the U.S. Forest Service, formed work parties that traveled to the mine. The work parties repaired damage done by vandals and cleaned and repaired buildings and structures that were in decay.

In early 2006, the U.S. Forest Service, headed by Ranger Jon Kazmierski, Lee Vining Visitor Center's director and recreation manager, showed renewed interest in the Log Cabin Mine. A plan was developed to construct a safe walking trail through the mine property by avoiding all hazardous areas. Interpretive panels depicting the original mine buildings and describing their function would be placed along the walking trail.

One example of decay and vandalism at the Log
Cabin Mine. (Cassidy Family Archives)

The sign erected by the work parties (just part
of their work). (Courtesy of MBHS)

The Eastern Sierra Interpretive Association (ESIA), headed by Debbe Eilts, agreed to help fund this project, and Eric Knight was commissioned to create the drawings for the panels. I was living in Arizona at the time and readily agreed to assist Eric with the accuracy of the panels.

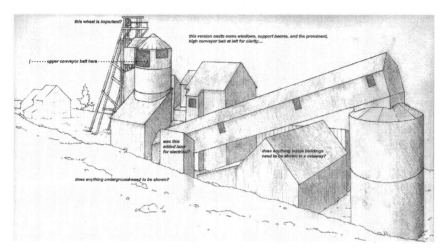

Eric's initial rough sketch of the mine. (Courtesy of USFS and Eastern Sierra Interpretive Association)

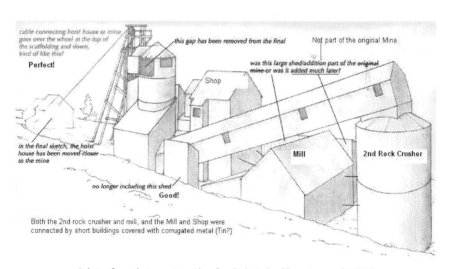

A lot of work to get to the final sketch. (Courtesy of USFS and Eastern Sierra Interpretive Association)

After numerous e-mails and phone calls between Eric and me, he produced an accurate sketch of the above-ground structures and the surrounding area.

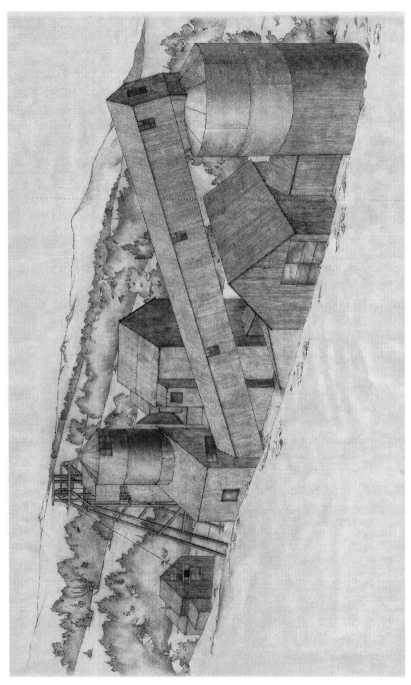

Eric's final sketch. What a job! This is the Log Cabin Mine as it actually was. A state-of-the-art gold mine at ten thousand feet. (Courtesy of USFS and Eastern Sierra Interpretive Association)

ESIA had also funded the portion of the project that involved Larry Arbanas of Earth River Productions traveling to Arizona to interview me for needed information for the interpretive panels. Larry and I had an in-depth interview concerning the mine structures and their function. Both Larry and I agreed that the four-hour interview was tiring but productive.

Meanwhile, the U.S. Forest Service was busy at the Log Cabin Mine doing necessary trail work and purchasing materials needed for the panels, such as wood, posts, and cement. The funding for this section of the project came from donations that the Forest Service acquired from the Mining Reclamation Fund, private parties, and a donation box in the Visitor Center in Lee Vining.

Unfortunately in 2007, mercury contamination was discovered in the soil around the Log Cabin Mine. The tailings residue left from the process of gold extraction probably caused this.

This soil contamination prevented the panels from being constructed along the trail. The project to build the interpretive walking trail was halted.

The Log Cabin Mine is a valuable historic site, but the decaying buildings and unmaintained grounds make it a dangerous place for unescorted exploration. Today, the mine is not open to the public.

But the history of the mine has been recorded and documented for all to learn from and enjoy. Thankfully, the U.S. Forest Service, headed by Ranger Jon Kazmierski and aided by the Eastern Sierra Interpretive Association and Debbe Eilts realized the importance of sharing this history. They persevered and have been able to bring the mine to the public via a movie presentation funded by ESIA and shown in the Mono Basin Visitor Center, entitled *The Log Cabin Mine, From Mine to Mint*.

I am extremely grateful to this team of experts who helped preserve the history, and to the special people who were part of my experience at the Log Cabin Mine. The first showing of *The Log Cabin Mine, From Mine to Mint* was in the fall of 2009, and it has become a routine presentation.

I feel that both my father and mother are present at every showing. To me, my parents really were the Log Cabin Mine.

Personal Reflections on the Log Cabin Mine

It is hard to put into words my feelings about my personal history of the Log Cabin Mine. I grew up at the mine. All the special people and my experiences there are still thankfully vivid in my memory. The mine is and was a truly magical place. I feel both my parents very close to me as I describe my experiences.

I took my wife, Robin, and our children to the Log Cabin Mine many times over the years. Robin's first visit, with our three children at the time, was in 1979. There was no mining activity, but good old Clarence Miller met us there. He was acting as caretaker, and of course, he still held to my father's strict standards. He kept the buildings so clean that you could eat off the cook shack floor. When my father was alive, you could eat off the floor of any of the buildings.

Beth, Scott, and Kris at the back of the superintendent's cabin, 1979. (Cassidy Family Archives)

Kris, Scott, and Beth in some ore cars in 1979. (Cassidy Family Archives)

Later in the eighties, when our family had grown to five children, three boys and two girls, we visited again. Sadly, Clarence was no longer there, and some buildings were showing their age, but I was proud to share this history with my family. I showed them all the remaining buildings and their functions. The boys, Scott, Jim, and Nick, and the girls, Elizabeth and Kristin, all had fun climbing on the remaining equipment, such as the Tucker Sno-Cat and the ore cars that were still on rails.

Many years earlier, my father, along with his crew, constructed a building at the top of the hill, which housed the Caterpillar and the Sno-Cat. They happily named this building the Cat House.

Jim Cassidy on the Sno-Cat during a family visit
to the mine (Cassidy Family Archives)

The girls liked to dress up in the mine hard hats and coats still left in the hoist house. Robin and I were kept busy trying to keep them away from the collar of the shaft to prevent them from falling in.

During this particular visit, we video recorded much of this activity. Throughout, the prominent dialog is asking (pleading, actually), "Please keep away from the shaft." All my kids gave me nasty looks for being too protective, but at least they did not fall down the shaft.

All the children loved to go to the top of the hill and look out over the beautiful view of Mono Lake and the Sierras. After enjoying the view, they would run gleefully with endless energy on the rim of the world.

It was on these trips that our kids learned the stories about their grandparents and the Log Cabin Mine.

I told them that it certainly did not look like it did when my father was alive. I feel very sad that they never had the chance to meet their grandfather. What stories he could have told them!

Visiting the mine became a family tradition. As each of our children has grown to adulthood and married, they have all taken their spouses up to the mine. Some have hiked and some have driven, but all have relived the stories that were told to them by their grandmother and me.

My personal history of the Log Cabin Mine is not complete without speaking of the following special places and people and the memories that make them meaningful to our family.

Special Places

The Sheep Corral

Many spots on the old Log Cabin Mine Road had gained nicknames over the years. One such spot is called the Sheep Corral because at one time there were remnants of old corrals made from aspen trees.

Other special sections include the long grade, because it is one steep, rocky son of a gun. (I edited the more appropriate term, as this book is rated for family audiences!) The runaround has a beautiful view of Highway 395 (some three thousand feet lower in elevation) all the way to June Mountain and beyond. You really do not run around the runaround!

The Sheep Corral has many other memories for me. Some people who knew my father were camped at the Sheep Corral that night we drove back to the mine after learning that my mother had survived her emergency surgery after my sister was born. We stopped to greet the campers, and my very relieved father proceeded to accept the campers' offer of an unlimited supply of bourbon in order to celebrate my mother's return to good health.

In the mountains, fathers often taught their children how to drive at a young age, and my training had taken place on the steep mine road. Without an automatic transmission, I really learned how to shift on the steep dirt roads. This was a good thing, because even though my father could really hold his liquor, it was the only time I ever saw him inebriated.

Thanks to his good instruction, I was able to navigate the truck up to the superintendent's cabin from the Sheep Corral—about three miles of steep road. Upon arriving, I amazingly got my father into the house and to bed. He was violently sick the rest of the night. The next morning, the only thing that was in the cupboard that I could fix was a can of oxtail soup. My father seemed very grateful for this meal and did hold it down, but it was a while before I saw him drink again. This story is told each time my family and I pass by the Sheep Corral, and I think fondly of my parents, the mine, and oxtail soup.

The Sheep Corral is also the steepest part of the old mine road (37 percent grade). This was a scary spot for truck drivers and passengers (Augie Hess, myself, etc.).

Years later, my wife, Robin, and I would hike to the mine from the ranger station. I would always announce, "This is the Sheep Corral, 37 percent grade, the steepest part of the road."

My wife always replied, "I don't need to know how steep it is because my legs can figure it out!" We would continue on to the mine, past the long grade and the runaround. As tired as we were after this long, steep hike, we were always exhilarated from a visit to the mine.

Through the years, my family and I walked the mine road many times. Even though Robin would complain about how steep it was, she grew to understand why we hiked instead of drove. She said she was fortunate to hear stories about the mine and its people at every turn and grade.

She came to appreciate what a unique man her father-in-law was and was saddened that he passed on before she was able to meet him. It was on these visits that she fell in love with the magic of the beauty of the Log Cabin Mine. After each hike to the mine, we would describe our hike to my mother, Carol, and she would talk about her many experiences. Robin liked picturing Carol (who had now become her mom) snowshoeing up the road, or spending her first winter there.

Our family's favorite story is of our mom sitting in that tent holding a .22 rifle across her lap. Carol was indeed a very special lady, and Robin expresses what a very lucky woman she was to have her as her mom.

Mom and me with her trusty .22, circa 1946. (Cassidy Family Archives)

Top of the Hill

A short distance up a dirt road from the last of the tailings ponds (residue from the processing of the ore) is what we called the Top of the Hill. This area overlooked the beautiful view of Mono Lake, which seemed almost straight down (it is probably about three miles).

The Top of The Hill with the Mono craters and a peek
at Mono Lake (Cassidy Family Archives)

Every Fourth of July, my father would retrieve a full box of Hercules blasting powder and take it to the Top of the Hill. He would dig a hole for the box and add a blasting cap and fuse. He really enjoyed rattling all the windows in the Mono Basin with this happy Fourth of July greeting. Yes, my father had a sense of humor.

Just about ready to light the fuse! Note the big grin. (Cassidy Family Archives)

THE NEW ROAD

My father saw the need for a new road to the mine that would be less steep and better accommodate the increased travel should the price of gold rise and lead to full operation of the mine once again. My father supervised all the construction, including the surveying for this road.

There was a portion of the new road along the top of the hill that passed right through groves of mountain mahogany bushes. These bushes were very dense and would branch out about three to four feet above the ground. During the summer when the road was constructed, I was the rod man during the surveying stage. This entailed crawling under the mountain mahogany with a one-hundred-foot tape and the rod, which I would poke up through the bushes at the one-hundred-foot mark. I would then move to the right or left as my father was sighting through his transit.

On one occasion, I left part of the tape at the last one-hundred-foot mark and had to crawl back to retrieve it. About halfway back, I discovered a timber rattlesnake sleeping about two feet to the side of my little crawl trail. As the snake began to wake up, I frantically collected some rocks on my hands and knees and did what I had to do to prevent a rattlesnake bite. Of course, this was just a minor risk as you consider the benefit of the new road.

The survey tape I used to crawl through the bushes along
with my dad's prospector's pick (on display at the Old
School House Museum). (Cassidy Family Archives)

As one leaves Highway 120 on the mine road, the new road branches to the right about a quarter of a mile up. The new road affords one a beautiful view of the meadows and groves of the Brand Morlan Lodge. As it nears the mine, the new road transverses the top of the hill and opens up to incredible vistas of Mono Lake. It is also very windswept (gusts up to 75 mph). On one of my and Robin's hikes to the mine on the new road, we literally had to hang on to each other to keep from being blown off the mountain and into Mono Lake.

Any time I either walk or drive the new road, I still marvel at the engineering and construction project my father carried out with the help of very few men.

Dad at the controls with Pete (right) and Clarence Miller with the Cat. The road builders, circa 1955. (Cassidy Family Archives)

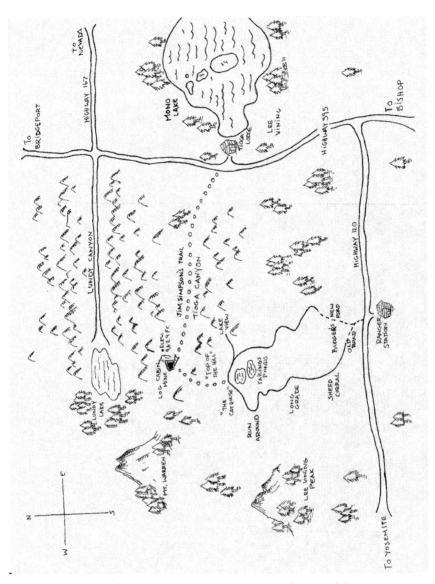

Hand-drawn map showing the location of some of the
"special places." (Courtesy of Kelli Baptista)

Special People

Frank Cassidy Sr.

My father was truly a renaissance man. He loved and excelled at every aspect of the mine experience.

I have been asked many times through the years if my father knew where all the gold was, and yes, he did!

My father's thirst for knowledge and adventure went beyond his job and contributed to who he was as a man and a father.

He sat on the Mono County School Board for a number of years. He supported the local educators and students and did his part to further the education system in Lee Vining.

He took up flying and obtained his private pilot's license. I remember one trip where he and I flew to Death Valley in the summertime, and we played golf at the Furnace Creek Golf Course. We had plenty of water because we were the only ones on the course, which was closed for the hot summer. My dad housed his plane at the Lee Vining airport. He and his mine crew had constructed a hanger, which was probably the first one built at the airport.

Dad's plane at the Lee Vining Airport. (Cassidy Family Archives)

In the early fifties, my dad became interested in taking 8 mm movies. He would edit and splice these movies into longer films. Since the film was without sound, he also filmed printed scroll describing the scenes and spliced them into the movies. The underground movies of the Log Cabin Mine are an example of his filming talent, and they are incorporated into the movie *The Log Cabin Mine, From Mine to Mint* that is shown at the Mono Basin Visitor Center.

My father, a true renaissance man, had many interests and talents, but his position as the superintendent of the Log Cabin Mine remained the most important to him. He continued to operate the mine through 1968 in a maintenance situation. His loyal employees, such as Pete Mathieu and Clarence Miller, remained with him. He also employed others, such as Jack Preston, who had previously worked many years for Venita McPherson, who was a very influential and successful Mono County supervisor. She also owned and operated the Mono Inn.

In 1968, at age fifty-eight, my father had a sudden attack of acute gastric bloating and pain while working at the mine. He was unable to drive, so Pete Mathieu got him down the hill to Lee Vining, where my mom joined them for the urgent drive to Bishop and Northern Inyo Hospital.

After some rapid tests, Dr. Sheldon performed emergency surgery. I was on my way back from Davis, California, where I was in my first year of veterinary school. Sadly, the surgery showed that my dad had colon cancer, which had progressed to his liver.

I arrived home and was able to spend time with him at the hospital. I remember shaving my dad (he liked to be clean shaven). They sent him home to Lee Vining with a colostomy and six months to live.

Soon after, he suffered a heart attack at home. I was able to get home to Lee Vining from school in time to help transport him back to the hospital. He seemed to be improving, but he died suddenly from a massive heart attack.

My father had a short life, but his star did indeed shine bright. He was a great man who touched many lives and hearts.

One of my prized possessions is the book *Men to Match My Mountains* written by Irving Stone. This book was originally given to my father in 1958 by my grandparents.

My father was truly a man to match the mountains and was the heart behind the Log Cabin Mine. My father was a man of many talents, and I loved him very much.

My dad's gravestone at Mono Lake Cemetery, July 2008. (Cassidy Family Archives)

PETE MATHIEU

Pete was my dad's foreman at the mine for many years (the Mathieu family were longtime residents of Benton in Mono County) and was the most even-tempered man that I have ever met. Pete and I were among the crew doing the handwork while my father ran the Caterpillar to build the new mine road.

Pete had quite a sense of humor. We encountered many rattlesnakes as we built the new road. Many people think that rattlesnakes can't live at ten thousand feet, but Pete and I definitely know that they do. Our usual procedure was to kill the rattlesnakes, removing the head with a shovel and pitching the remains off the road. After one such beheading, Pete yelled loudly, "Watch out!" This mock warning made me jump ten feet in the air. I still remember Pete's big grin.

Before Pete's marriage to Lily La Braque (the La Braque family were longtime residents of the Mono Basin), he lived at the bunkhouse of the Log Cabin Mine. One evening, the phone line was abuzz. A phone line had previously been constructed, connecting the mine, the superintendent's cabin, our house in Lee Vining, the halfway house, which was a small tin building on the old mine road, and would eventually extend to the Mathieu household in Lee Vining. Pete had been saving money religiously for his upcoming wedding to Lily and had somehow misplaced his stash. Everyone was put to work madly looking for the money. It was eventually found, and the wedding took place as planned on July 5, 1949. Shortly thereafter, my parents, Frank Cassidy Sr. and Carol Cassidy, extended a formal invitation to the newly married couple to be the guests of honor at a wedding banquet held at the Log Cabin Mine. Lily says that a great time was had by all, and a delicious turkey dinner had been prepared by Mr. and Mrs. Rasmussen, who were the mine cooks at the time.

Pete and Lily at the wedding banquet at the mine,
July 1949. (Courtesy of Lily Mathieu)

Pete, Lily and family were a vital part of the Log Cabin Mine for years.

Pete also had the well-deserved title of the best trout fisherman in Mono County. My father had many talents, but trout fishing was not one of them. Pete deserves credit for teaching me to fish.

On one occasion, he took me to Lower Sardine Lake. I can remember going to his house in Lee Vining before sunup. Pete had coffee, and I had hot chocolate. The trail to Lower Sardine is long, steep, and arduous, especially for a little kid. Pete could see I was getting weary during the last part of the hike, and he actually carried me and my gear the last few yards to the lake. I will always remember and admire Pete's strength.

Pete usually had a Camel cigarette in his mouth. I remember him happily flicking the cigarette butts out into the water and watching the trout fight over them. Needless to say, we "limited out," or reached our quota of fish (fifteen at that time) very quickly. Fortunately, the trip back was downhill.

Years later, I took my family on the very same hike. I was telling them the story of Pete carrying me the last few yards, and they looked at me and said in unison, "Carry me!" Well, five kids made that an impossible task, but I did end up carrying all the gear and fond thoughts of Pete to the lake.

The Mathieu family got an unexpected Christmas gift, circa 1956. Pete was to snowshoe down from the mine, early on Christmas Eve to join his family in Lee Vining, but he did not show up. A major snowstorm had knocked out the one phone line to the mine so his family was not able to contact him. This single phone line was the lifeline between the miners and their families in Lee Vining.

An all-out search was initiated, which included the Civil Air Patrol. Bob Symonds, from his flying service in Lone Pine, piloted the plane that spotted Pete safely snowshoeing down on Christmas Day. Heavy snows prevented the plane from landing, so Bob wrote on a roll of toilet paper that Pete was okay and on his way down. He then dropped this missile to a worried and frantic Mathieu family in Lee Vining. Thankfully, this story had a happy ending!

In 1968, just before my father's funeral service, Pete gently took me to Mono Lake Cemetery, where he and other men were preparing my father's resting place. I will always be grateful for his kindness and sensitivity at that very difficult time. After the funeral, a wake was held at my parents' house in Lee Vining (which is still beautifully maintained by the Logan family).

Augie Hess, in a starched white shirt, was the bartender at the wake.

The indestructible Augie Hess, sportsman and gentleman, with his 1937 Cord on his ninety-fifth birthday, October 25, 2009, at Bishop, California. (Courtesy of Vineca Hess)

Pete left all of us who loved him for a better place in 1979. He suffered a massive heart attack while chopping wood. He left behind a fine family, and I lost a dear friend. Pete truly was my buddy.

Lee Vining people are special, and I am proud to have my roots there.

Clarence Miller

The Garbutt/Hathaway family had asked my dad to hire Clarence and to bring him and his wife, Eloise (who was related to the Hathaways), to live and work at the mine.

Their trip to the mine occurred in the winter, and Eloise, who was a bountiful woman, rode in the Tucker Sno-Cat, which was routinely used for winter travel to the mine. The Sno-Cat bogged down during this particular trip to the mine due to the generous load. This was an unusual occurrence, and once corrected, they all arrived safely at the mine.

Methods of winter travel at the mine. (Cassidy Family Archives)

Frank Cassidy Sr. at the controls of the Tucker Sno-Cat. (Cassidy Family Archives)

Pete Mathieu, foreman of the Log Cabin Mine with the
Tucker Sno-Cat. (Cassidy Family Archives)

Clarence and Eloise lived in the cabin across the wash from the back of the cook shack. Clarence took to mine living, but Eloise did not and left soon after she arrived. Clarence moved to quarters in the cook shack, and he was a valued worker at the mine for many years. He idolized my father and would do anything for him.

The Millers' house. (Cassidy Family Archives)

My father trained Clarence to be the hoist operator. I can still remember when I was working at the mine, standing on that skip to be lowered four hundred feet down, and looking straight in the windows of the hoist house to see Clarence with that traditional toothpick in his mouth. He was a picture of concentration. My only thought was, *Clarence, please let me down easy*, and he always did.

Clarence Miller at work. (Cassidy Family Archives)

After my father's death and the subsequent donation of the mine property by the Garbutt/Hathaway families to the Boy Scouts of America, Clarence stayed on as caretaker of the property. One summer, I took my family for a tour of the mine, and Clarence met us at the cook shack door. It was as clean as my father had kept it, and Clarence proudly wanted us all to have a glass of water that my father had always proclaimed to be the best-tasting water a person would ever have. He was right, and I know my father was smiling.

BODIE SAM

Bodie Sam was one of the Asian cooks my father hired. What a character! He would sit out back of the cook shack in the evening and shoot sage hens with a .22 rifle. (This was highly illegal even for those times.) He called the sage hens "brown chickie." He claimed they were good for "boy" (me) and would serve them regularly. He was also a good baker. I remember once when I had the flu and I was in the superintendent's cabin, I looked out the window to see Bodie Sam, who was a rotund man, trudging up the path from the cook shack at the mine. He had a pie in each hand. Bodie was dressed in his starched white uniform and hat. When he arrived, he said, "Pie good for boy," and they sure were.

I'm waiting for Bodie Sam at the steps of the superintendent's cabin, circa 1947. (Cassidy Family Archives)

MIKE THE DOG

My parents obtained Mike for me in Lee Vining when I was about nine years old. He was a lovable brown and white rat terrier puppy. Mike became a mine dog because of his propensity for chasing cars in Lee Vining, even after being hit several times. Mike definitely had nine lives. He survived not only the cars but also being accidently locked in one of the vacant Banta cabins in Lee Vining at the Lake View Lodge.

The length of time that he was locked up varies greatly from my version of nine days to Don Banta's version of two hours. But I did find Mike looking out the window of that empty cabin after returning from a trip to Los Angeles. I still jokingly accuse Don Banta of locking him in there on purpose, and it brings a laugh every time. Don Banta continues to be a valued friend.

At the mine, Mike would wag his tail and bark madly at the opening of the mine shaft as the skip was lowered down. He would stand right on the edge, and I never lost my fear of him falling in. Thankfully, he never did.

Mike and me at the mine, circa 1947. (Cassidy Family Archives)

Mike slept in the framing shed in the warm sawdust. One spring, a large bear had to have been very hungry for a little dog. The bear actually tore through the side of the framing shed to get at Mike, who somehow wedged himself under some steps to avoid being the bear's dinner. Mike lived to be eighteen years old and was my great little companion.

The steps in the framing shed that were Mike's refuge
from the hungry bear. (Cassidy Family Archives)

This is a poem about Mike I wrote in school, around 1947, which Carol
typed and saved for many years:

> *Mike*
> *Mike's not pretty, his ears don't match*
> *And under his chin there's a white patch*
> *And one of his ears is scarred*
> *Where the neighbor's cat clawed him too hard*
> *But he can do tricks and play dead*
> *And he almost learned to stand on his head*
> *He'd never win a dog show prize*
> *But he's a wonder for his size*
> *And I wouldn't trade Mike for a French Poodle pup*
> *Whose eyes weren't funny*
> *And whose ears stood up!*

DALLAS BURGER

Dallas had purchased the Brand Morlan Lodge property, which was situated on the old road to the Log Cabin Mine. L. C. Brand had purchased this land in 1913. Mr. Brand was an avid fisherman and developed the 160 acres. He built the lodge and even a nine-hole golf course.

Mr. Morlan inherited the development in 1927. Dallas and his wife, Miriam, acquired the property in 1945 from Mr. Morlan's relatives.

Originally, the old road went only as far as the lodge, and it was later extended to go the full distance to the Log Cabin Mine. In the early days, the road afforded Jim Simpson an easier way to transport supplies than straight up Tioga Canyon.

I knew Dallas well, and he was a fascinating man. Dallas and my father developed a mutual respect for one another. He and my father had a gentlemen's agreement about the road because it passed through his property on the way to the mine.

Dallas was a Lockheed engineer who, during World War II, was literally locked up at the Lockheed facility with three other engineers until they could come up with a solution to combat the German ME-I09 fighter, which was dominating the U.S. fighters. They emerged with the plan for the P-38. This, along with the P-51, regained U.S. dominance in the skies.

Dallas and his family used the property to escape the pressure that accompanied his job in Los Angeles. As the road was not open during the winter, the Burgers and guests, usually other Lockheed engineers with their families, arrived in the warmer months.

When working on his property, one of the first things Dallas did was take his shirt off. My father and I would pass through twice a day, to and from the mine, during the summer months, and it was rare to see Dallas with his shirt on. Dallas was outside a lot because he loved the wildlife on the property, which he eventually developed into a bird and game refuge.

It was not unusual to see many deer and a wide variety of birds as we passed through. Of course, Dallas protected them by posting many No Hunting signs.

When my wife, Robin, and I pass through the Brand Morlan meadow on our walks to the mine, we look for the sign posted on one of the Aspen groves, which reads Robin's Grove. My wife particularly loves that grove, and she likes to think that Dallas named the grove for her.

Dallas Burger. What a gentleman. (Courtesy of MBHS)

The Burgers and Cassidys became good friends, and the Burgers were a welcome addition to Mono County for many years.

My parents, along with my sister, Kathleen, and me, had joined Dallas and his wife, Miriam, many times for dinner in the lodge dining room during the years 1949–55. Sadly, Dallas and Miriam are no longer with us, but their memories live on.

They both had special wooden rocking chairs on the porch of the lodge from where they could better view the scenery and wildlife.

In 2009, Robin and I packed our lunch, parked our truck on the mine road across from the ranger station, and hiked up to the lodge. It was locked up, but we were able to sit in those special rockers with reverence, courtesy of Dallas and Miriam, while we ate our lunch. We were very grateful for that opportunity to enjoy our lunch on the porch of the Brand Morlan Lodge.

Patricia Keith Esborg

My cousin Pat grew up in Southern California, but our families would often get together during the holidays and other visits. Pat and I are very close in age. She was a city girl, and I was a mountain boy. She was able to spend summers with my family at the mine. She absolutely loved it and gained an early appreciation for the outdoors and the High Sierras. Our favorite pastime was mining our own operation, which we dug by hand some yards from the superintendent's house. We didn't find any gold, but we had a good time and avoided cave-ins.

Pat and me at the bus. (Cassidy Family Archives)

I'm standing proudly by my mine. My helper, cousin Pat, is missing from the photo. Note the sturdy gallis frame (circa 1947). (Cassidy Family Archives)

Pat may have been the first female allowed into the underground of the Log Cabin Mine. She vividly remembers suiting up to go down the shaft, and she and I (circa 1948), accompanied by our protector, Pete Mathieu, rode that rickety cage down to the wet lowest level of the mine (the drain tunnel), where we got to do a little exploring. Pat's experiences at the mine seemed to help shape her life. She still loves to explore caves and experience the rough and tumble of life.

She chose to work in the industrial ward of Good Samaritan Hospital while in nurses' training. Other student nurses shied away from the ward because of the tough construction men there, but Pat loved it and was up for the challenge.

Pat had a successful career in psychiatric nursing and later obtained her doctorate in sociology. She still actively conducts a private practice specializing in individual and couples therapy.

Pat now lives in Maryland with her husband, Svend. They have both been back to the Mono Basin and the Log Cabin Mine, and both say their heart and souls are there.

Kathleen Cassidy Blackbern

My sister, Kathleen, is eleven years younger than I am and has her own personal history of the Log Cabin Mine.

Mom, Kathleen, and Mike at the mine (circa 1950). (Cassidy Family Archives)

After my mother's recovery from surgery shortly after Kathleen's birth in 1949, she and Kathleen returned to Lee Vining. Kathleen would become a country girl. She attended Lee Vining Elementary School and graduated from Lee Vining High School in 1967.

Mrs. Hasty, the wife of my old high school principal, taught her in grades one through three. This was in a new building that was erected just east of the old grammar school. She attended grades four through six in the same building I had, but she did not experience Mrs. Archer's ruler action that I had in third grade. (Apparently, her fifth-grade teacher more than made up for that.)

Kathleen attended grades seven and eight in the same building where I attended high school. The sign above the front door of the school read "Lee Vining Elem School." Kathleen was in the first class in the new Lee Vining High School, which was constructed at the north end of town. Her graduating class of 1967 had twenty-seven students. Kathleen was a classmate and friend of Vineca Hess, Augie's daughter. Vineca is an active member of the Mono Basin Historical Society, and she was the first person who pointed her finger at me and commanded, "You have to write a book."

Rural living continued to pose problems, though. When Kathleen was eight years old, she developed pneumonia and had to be rushed to Bishop. The lower elevation helped her breathing somewhat, but she was hurriedly driven to Los Angeles to our family doctor. In Kathleen's words, "I almost croaked." She recovered, though, and returned to Lee Vining.

Her next adventure, at age nine, was at Mammoth Mountain, where her skis got tangled up in rope tow number one. The result was a fractured femur. Since my father was working at the mine, our mom had to rush to Mammoth and then transport Kathleen to Bishop for the fracture repair. Yes, both mother and daughter had to be tough. Kathleen was tough, but Mom made that her last ski trip.

Kathleen and I fondly remember one summer of many family picnics in Simpson Meadow. I was twenty-one, and Kathleen was ten years old. We would cook steaks over an open fire, and my father and I would toast Jim Simpson, Frank Garbutt, and a few others. This usually led to a shooting competition using my father's trusty .38 and targets pasted on a pine tree. My mother would become somewhat nervous even in spite of her .22 rifle experience. We generally had a great time in beautiful surroundings, with Jim Simpson's old cabin only a few feet away.

Kathleen and I both still talk about the trip down the mine road in the dark after those picnics. We would ride in a seat in the back of the Blue Beetle, which was that old GI four-by-four truck that my father had purchased for the mine and painted blue. There was no roof on the back, so my sister and I were treated to a great view of the brilliant stars over the Sierras all the way down the road to Lee Vining.

The trips to Simpson Meadow were not the only picnics that my sister remembers. My father's idea of the ideal picnic was to travel from Lee Vining to one of the old mining areas, such as Bodie or Aurora. There, he would pluck down the cooking grate in the middle of some sagebrush, preferably after a rain. My father taught us all to love the smell of sagebrush after a rain.

Our dad would never be without his prospector's pick, and he would happily roam the area, examining the various rock formations. Apparently, you can never take the study of geology out of the miner.

There was a rule about not allowing females to go down into the mine. Cousin Pat had previously broken that rule, but my sister remembers Dad sneaking her down on a weekend. Reliable Clarence Miller was the hoist operator. Imagine this young girl all decked out in heavy coat, rubber boots, hard hat, and battery pack on her waist attached to the light on her hat. Boy, does she remember that trip! What an experience.

I am not sure whether my mother knew about Kathleen's adventure, but perhaps that is one of the reasons that my father sneaked her down into the mine.

Kathleen and I still enjoy reminiscing about our experiences together at the Log Cabin Mine. Kathleen proudly displays one of the original mine phones in her home.

One of the mine phones proudly displayed on Kathleen's
wall. (Courtesy of Kathleen Blackbern)

Kathleen now resides with her own family in Visalia, California, and continues to be actively involved in the administrative section of the Visalia School System. She has helped many children (especially disadvantaged ones) and is a very caring person.

CAROL CASSIDY (BAUER)

My mother was a special lady, whether with a .22 rifle across her lap or hosting a dinner party. She always held herself with grace and sophistication. She loved what she referred to as her peek at Mono Lake from the porch of the superintendent's cabin at the Log Cabin Mine.

As well as working at the mine, she held several jobs as a bookkeeper in Lee Vining for local businesses in the fifties and sixties, and they valued her highly.

Even after my father's death, she continued these positions, and the community held her in the highest respect.

I also hold her in the highest respect. As I grow older, I realize the special qualities that she showed all through her long life. She was truly a shining star.

She was courageous. Imagine her ready to take on wild animals in a tent in the Simpson Meadow to protect her baby.

She was a great mom. She researched the college preparation curriculum at UC Berkeley and UCLA in the early fifties and then worked with Mr. C. Gerald Hasty, then principal of Lee Vining High School, to establish that curriculum at the school, so that I could qualify for admittance to the University of California. She was the reason that I was able to attend UC Berkeley and that subsequently Lee Vining High School became accredited.

She loved reminiscing about adventures. My mom used to love to tell the story of Twinkle Toes. As a youngster, I had somehow acquired a cat that I called Twinkle Toes. He was a big male that loved to roam at night. She would tell people that I knocked at the front door one morning holding Twinkle Toes behind my back and said, "Mom, whatever you do, don't look!" Twinkle Toes had evidently been shot and appeared at our doorstep with one eye hanging out of its socket. I knew that I had a great mom, but cats were not her favorite thing, especially one that was maimed so badly.

She never did look, but she loved to tell the story of how she knew I would become a veterinarian because I somehow removed the hanging eye, placed Twinkle Toes in a box, and nursed him back to health.

She was correct about my becoming a veterinarian. In later years, she enjoyed us telling her the story about Roy Rogers singing "Happy Trails" to Robin in the kennels of our veterinary surgical hospital. (Robin was my surgical technician, and we had spent seven long hours in surgery repairing Roy's dog, Sam. Sam had been badly injured during a break-in at Roy's museum.)

My mom was independent. After my father's passing, she chose to stay in Lee Vining, the area that she loved, and continue the bookkeeping jobs in town. She also took a job at the June Lake Public Utilities District. She drove between Lee Vining and June Lake every day by herself for nine years. At the time, the road was only two lanes and could be very dangerous, especially in the winter.

In 1977, she met and married Roland Bauer, a police officer from the Los Angeles Police Department who had retired to June Lake. She was active in many community activities in both Lee Vining and June Lake.

Carol loved the Log Cabin Mine and the time she and my father had there. At various community events, she would show the 8 mm movies my father had taken and speak about the mine. In the late eighties, she moved to Bishop for Roland's heath. She busied herself with Bishop community activities and bridge playing. She also continued her passion to keep the history of the Log Cabin Mine alive by showing the 8 mm film and speaking at community functions. She had fourteen happy adventure-filled years with Roland before he passed away.

Carol Cassidy (Bauer) still snowshoeing at sixty-two years young! (Cassidy Family Archives)

She was one tough lady. I don't know if she would approve that I describe her as tough as nails, but I believe that the term definitely fits.

Some time after Roland's passing, she met Fred Pratt and a happy companionship developed. She once again lost a partner after Fred's sudden passing.

Robin once said to her she didn't know how Mom could withstand so many losses and still face life with such eternal optimism. Mom's response was, "But, dear, look at all the wonderful happenings and adventure I have had in my life."

While in Bishop, Robin and I visited and shopped for her weekly, but Mom always made a point to ask us if we could work around her bridge days. Of course, we were happy to do so.

Unfortunately, Carol fell and fractured her upper arm in many places. While at the Northern Inyo Hospital emergency room, she was taken for X-rays. Robin and I accompanied her. The radiology technician was attempting to move Mom to the proper position for the X-rays. She never once whimpered. Instead, she calmly stated, "I might have really done something." Moreover, indeed she had. Carol suffered a severely broken upper arm, but as usual, I never heard her complain of pain or her loss of mobility.

When Carol was at Northern Inyo Hospital, there was quite some confusion over whose mother she actually was since both Robin and I referred to her as "my mom." When we were asked which one of us actually belonged to Carol, both Robin and I answered in unison: "Me." Well, we cleared up the confusion, but it definitely summed up our mom.

During my mom's final days on this earth (ninety-three years young), Robin and I would sit at her bedside and remind her of those better days and that it was okay to be joining Dad for those martinis. One afternoon when we suggested that he had been waiting a long time for her to fix him another martini, she smiled peacefully and her brilliant blue eyes sparkled. She passed to a better place later that evening . I like to believe that she and my father shared martinis that night and toasted their loved ones and their life at the Log Cabin Mine.

Carol's qualities, including courage, grace, sophistication, independence, and toughness, live on in her six grandchildren and great-grandchildren. Fortunately, she was able to be influential in their lives.

Her memorial bench at Mono Lake Cemetery reads "From hardship to triumph, always an upbeat attitude." No truer words were ever spoken.

The angel that stands behind the bench represents how Carol guards all she loves. She truly is my guardian angel, and I love her very much.

My mom's memorial at Mono Lake Cemetery,
July 2008. (Cassidy Family Archives)

Together, it was my mom and dad who made the Log Cabin Mine such
a magical place, with a personal history to match no other.

About the Author

Frank C. Cassidy Jr., DVM, (also known as Nick Cassidy to the people of Lee Vining) was born in 1938 in Southern California and spent most of his youth at the Log Cabin Mine and Lee Vining, California.

He graduated from Lee Vining High School in 1955 (graduating class of five students) and attended the University of California, Berkeley, from 1955 to 1959.

Frank's father, Frank Cassidy Sr., was the general superintendent of the Log Cabin Mine from 1939 until his death in 1968. Frank Jr. lived with his family at the mine during the summers until he entered high school. During this time, he was exposed to the mine at full operation.

During high school, he helped with some of the above-ground duties.

Frank Jr. was employed at the Log Cabin Mine while at home away from college during the summers. His duties included those both above-ground and underground. He is probably one of the very few people left to have actually worked underground at the Log Cabin Mine.

He spent time in the U.S. Air Force and later worked as a lineman for PG&E in the Bay Area. He eventually returned to school at the University of California, Davis, in 1967. He graduated with his doctorate in Veterinary Medicine in 1971, just as his mother predicted.

He went on to a three-year surgical residency at the University of Minnesota.

Upon returning to California, he owned and operated Jurupa Hills Animal Hospital, a veterinary surgical hospital in Southern California, for twenty-five years.

While in Southern California, he and his family visited the Eastern Sierras and the Log Cabin Mine frequently.

Frank and his wife, Robin, have five grown children, four grandchildren (and counting), and a four-legged baby named Smokey (one very spoiled miniature schnauzer).

Keeping with family tradition, each of their children return to the Eastern Sierras with their families and include visits to the Log Cabin Mine.

Frank and Robin now divide their time between Rio Vista, California, (near the Sacramento Delta), and Lee Vining.

Frank Cassidy Sr. (right) with two of his miners. (Cassidy Family Archives)